A Holliston Oath to Support and Defend

BOBBY BLAIR
The "Mayor of Mudville"

A Holliston Oath to Support and Defend

Text, cover photo and photos on pages 9, 17, 35, 41, 45, 49, 61, 99, 107, 111, 113
© Bobby Blair.

Designer/Art Director – LisaThompsonGraphicDesign.com
Editor – PeruzziCommunications.com

Library of Congress Control Number: 9781941573273
ISBN: 2021907181

Published by Damianos Publishing
Saxonville Mills
2 Central Street, Studio 152
Framingham, MA 01701
www.DamianosPublishing.com

Produced through Silver Street Media by Bridgeport National Bindery,
Agawam, MA USA

First printed 2021

Acknowledgments

To all who came forth and contributed photos of their loved ones for this second book about Holliston veterans – thank you!

To Mary Greendale, who started my writing obsession with her newfangled online newspaper called *Holliston Net News* way back in 2005, by saying to me, "Maybe you can write a little weekly farm column about what's coming in from the fields." See what you started.

To Matthew Payton, owner of Holliston's Bit Bull Computer Service, this baby boomer couldn't have pulled this book off without your technical help.

To the folks in the Holliston Lions Club, little could you realize that after seventy-five years, your organization's *Holliston Servicemen's News* newsletter would be such a historical treasure.

To neighbor and Town Historian Joanne Hulbert, your prodding, encouragement, and wealth of information are endless.

When little was left but hope back in 1997, along came a man (Bill G.) to help me with my addiction to John Barleycorn. You saved my life, Bill, and made the twelve promises come true.

To the folks at Damianos Publishing, Lynne, Lisa, and Brett, you made a dream come true, not once but twice, in the same year no less.

To the families who have sent off loved ones to our nation's defense, your sacrifice is noted.

To the big guy upstairs I call God, I'm not sure this is what you intended me to do, but you did bring me back from that distant place, so I gave it a go.

Introduction

After having written my first book *A Holliston Call to Duty* it became readily apparent that a second book was needed to highlight the sacrifices of Holliston veterans. While I didn't wish to focus on any particular war in this book, *A Holliston Oath to Support and Defend*, a wealth of tidbits and leads would come from the Lions Club publication the *Holliston Servicemen's News*. Hence the number of World War II veterans from "The Greatest Generation" in this book. The *Holliston Servicemen's News* had a column devoted to small town Holliston (with a population hovering around 3,350 in 1945) with short snippets under the heading "Local Scenes". One typical example: "Mrs. Harry Jagger, Grove Street, while up town shopping, slipped on the icy sidewalk in front of Reemie's Drug Store and suffered a broken ankle."

The two-sided newsletter, eight copies in all, from November 1944 through July-August 1945 devoted the rest of the newsletter to "Briefs About the Boys" (as well as some women who also served). For example: "2nd Lt. Martha Honey Welch is living in a hut in France as a nurse and is expected home soon". While the locations of service members stateside was often revealed, the locations of those serving overseas would be more vague. Remember, "loose lips sink ships". Although the newsletter holds a plethora of names, time has taken its toll and most are now gone. Holliston has as of March 2021 only fourteen living World War II veterans.

Having grown up in town was a plus for me when connecting the next generation to deceased veterans, even when names changed due to marriage. In one instance I tracked down a great-grandson in Colorado of one of the town's World War I veterans who had no memory or photo of his ancestor. Fortunately, in my pile of photos, I did. Imagine my surprise after snooping around a bit, to learn a facility was located at 55 Prospect Street to retrain war dogs after World War II. I lived a mere three doors down on Prospect Street and played as a kid in the barn that housed those dogs. Could it have been coincidence that the man who purchased that property in 1950, Joseph Kempton, was also a World War II veteran, who to my astonishment had written a book called *Dynamite On The Desk*. Kempton's travails take you from D-Day through the Battle of the Bulge. I mean, who knew these things? I did a double take when former childhood neighbor John Bresnahan laid his dad's (Warren "Presty" Bresnahan) World War II scrapbook book on my kitchen table. Warren had been part of a team to escort Japanese officials to the *USS Missouri* in Tokyo Bay for the surrender of Japan on September 2, 1945.

Once again, *A Holliston Oath to Support and Defend* barely scratches the surface of those from this town called Holliston who held up their right hand upon entry into the military and repeated the words "To support and defend the Constitution of the United States against all enemies, foreign and domestic". If for no other reason, this book will keep for posterity the names and faces of those who have passed our way.

Richard Blodgett

Pvt. Richard H. Blodgett was a student when he enlisted to Holliston's Company B, Sixteenth Regiment, Volunteer Infantry on August 13, 1862. Wounded at Gettysburg on July 2-3, 1863, he would re-enlist on December 23, 1863 and again be wounded at the Battle of the Wilderness in Virginia on May 6, 1864. Blodgett would be transferred to the Eleventh Massachusetts Infantry, Company E. The Blodgett family home was located at 2 Smith Row.

APRIL 6 1917 TO MAY 23 1923

ROBERT H ADAMS
JEROME B ALTIMUS
ALBERT C AMES
TIMOTHY G AMES
JOSEPH S ASHWORTH
WILLIAM J BACKSHALL
CLIFFORD W BACKUS
ELMER L W BARRY
FREDERICK L BARRY
ALDEN M BARTLETT
CHARLES O BARTLETT
LESLIE R BARTLETT
STEPHEN W BARTLETT
LOUIS R BESOZZI
EDWARD B BLIZZARD
ALFRED J BRAY
THOMAS A BRAY
ALBERT C BRISSETTE
HENRY E CAREY
LLEWELLYN A CHAPMAN
ERNEST H CHASE

FRANK GALLANT
JOSEPH A GALLANT
JOSEPH A GALLERANI
LOUIS GALLERANI
*HAROLD W GALLISON
ERNEST G GATES
LOUIS GEORGE
STEPHEN GEORGE
THOMAS A GOOCH
MAX GOTZ
JAMES J HAMILTON
WALTER P HATCH
DENNIS W HEFFERNAN
WILLIAM J HENDERSON
ALBERT L HERRICK
CHARLES L HICKEY
WALTER D HIGGINS
HENRY HILCHEY
HENRY P HOLBROOK
STEPHEN P HONEY
GEORGE B HOWARTH

JEROME J MOORE
FRED R MORSE
WALTER R MOYNIHAN
HENRY L MURRAY
NORMAN W MYRER
BENJAMIN NAIMON
MORRIS NAIMON
JOHN E NEWELL
GEORGE W NOTTAGE
FRED J O CONNELL
WILLIAM P O'GRADY
JAMES L O'LEARY
WILLIAM O'NEIL
JOHN N OSBORNE
LEROY J PARKER
NEWELL A PEAVEY
CARL L PHIPPS
CHESTER D PHIPPS
JOSEPH L PHIPPS
WARREN H PIDGEON
HAROLD PLAISTOWE

World War I honor roll at town hall

"ATTENTION!

The fire alarm at Holliston will be blown at 5 o'clock a.m. on Tuesday, June 5, 1917, ten successive times announcing military enrollment. The board of registrars will be in session at the selectmen's room from 5:30 a.m. until 9 p.m.

All liable under the following conditions must register: Every male who has reached his 21st birthday and who has not yet reached his 31st birthday on June 5, 1917, must register on that day, whether a voter or not. There is no exemption from registration except for those actually in the military service of the United States.

Registration does not mean you will have to go to war. You may be exempted later from actual service, but if you are within the ages specified you must register. Your place of registration is the regular polling place in your home precinct; if you do not know where this is, ask your city or town clerk.

Charles F. Gettemy
Director of Military Enrollment for Massachusetts"

William O'Grady

Bill O'Grady was a Winthrop Street resident and World War I veteran. O'Grady served as a commander for the local American Legion Post 47. Bill is shown here with his daughters Nancy and Ellen, who were members of the Legion Drum and Bugle Corps. O'Grady also served as the town's postmaster in the late 1930s and early 1940s.

Alden Leland

Lt. Alden Leland was a member of the 304th Regiment. The unit was created primarily with men from Connecticut as part of the Seventy-sixth Infantry Division on August 29, 1917, at Camp Devens, Massachusetts, for the purpose of fighting Imperial Germany in World War I. Colonel Joseph S. Herron was appointed as the unit's first commander and set sail with the unit from Boston Harbor on July 7, 1918. The unit arrived in England, rested, then crossed the English Channel for Le Havre, France, on July 27, 1918. Once in place in France, the unit served as a replacement regiment, providing officers and soldiers to the units currently fighting on the front line. After the war, Leland would conduct his business, Alden Leland Insurance, from a very small building next to Aubuchon Hardware (present day Fiske's Store) in the town center. The small building had no bathroom and loosened floor boards would reveal the brook below that runs under Washington Street to answer anyone's call of nature.

Harold E. Shippee

A letter home from Harold:

"Hello boys,

I just received a card your clerk George Chesmore sent. It sure seems good to hear from the old town once in a while. I wonder if you are kept on the jump as much as the organizations are over here, ha ha. A little different I am afraid, it is really a different fire. The yell over here is instead of 'fire,' it is 'gas,' and then, well all there is to do is to put on our disguise which is a great protection. A few of the boys are in the hospital from being gassed but will be all right in a few days, I guess. The other day we witnessed an air raid and battle in the air in which 142 planes took active part and believe me it was thrilling. The report came in today that ten Boche machines were shot down, in fact we saw three come down in flames.

We are expected to be relieved before many days now, to go back to a rest camp to re-organize and fill up with equipment, let's hope they keep going. We are all feeling pretty good and if it would only dry up a bit there would be a great change in all. The food we get is good and plenty so as long as a shell don't come over with our name on it, why worry? Well, boys, this is about all I can or rather dare to write so will say 'so-long.'

Yours respectfully,

Mech. Harold E. Shippee AEF
October 21, 1918"

World War I vets in 1976

The last gathering of Holliston's World War I vets at town hall on November 11, 1976. Present but not pictured was Fred Miller, who became ill during the photo shoot.

Charles Maguire

Charles Maguire and his wife Margurette pose in front of Mudville's Arch Street Bridge. Maguire was a World War I veteran and an adult leader for the American Legion's Drum and Bugle Corps. Maguire was employed at the bowling alley at 9 Green Street, which later housed the Ty-Car Manufacturing Company.

Fred Miller

From *The Framingham News,* 1944:

"Chairman Fred Miller of the Holliston committee on public safety thought so much of the activities of the disaster and relief committee, and its energetic chairman, that he appointed them in a body to his committee. With a fully trained staff of competent first aid workers in the group, a first aid station, and ambition to expand with further activities for the public interest, it had the wholehearted support of the entire town. This section of the committee on public safety would instill in the minds of the Holliston public that if the bombs come, if the hurricane roars, or if the flood waters rise, there is an efficient unit of their fellow citizens ready and trained to furnish them with adequate assistance.

May it also be remembered by Holliston residents that if no doctor or nurse is available during any household emergency, the committee has made arrangements whereby the public may dial 444 on the telephone and Miss Celia Haley, police and fire dispatcher will put them immediately in touch with one of the trained staff of first aiders."

Miller would go on to teach high school upperclassmen to operate the search light on top of the hose tower at Central Station in search of enemy planes. While Miller may be best remembered as an educator, he was also a World War I veteran.

Newspaper clipping of the Cox family, The Boston Herald,
July 29, 1944

In this photo, the Cox family meets in England. Left to right Capt. Ernest Cox, his father, Lt. Col. Lawrence Cox, and his sister Lt. Christine Cox.

In late April of 1945, Christine wrote her mother in Holliston.

"As I told you I've been transferred again and am now living in a 4-girl tent in the middle of a big muddy and plowed wheat field. This is an all tent affair too and very similar to the other. We work eight hours, have eight off then go on for eight again, so that you can see there's nothing very regular about our hours. We saw an awful thing today – in a place about thirty miles farther from the front than we are was a big old building in the middle of a cleared field. Here the Germans had crowded all the Russian prisoners and a few Americans and others, and after pouring gasoline on them they burned them. This was a few days ago and the fire was still burning when the American military government took over the town. Every civilian in that town has to bury one body properly, mound the grave and place a cross on it and keep fresh flowers on it indefinitely. Over 500 have been recovered already and there's hardly a dent. That's the straight dope – we've seen it and want you at home to know about it."

Alfred "Camel" Kampersal

From the *Holliston Servicemen's News* – November 1944:

"Pfc. Alfred Kampersal, Engineers Aviation Battalion, and Pvt. Ralph Sherman, Q.M. Truck Corps, met in France and report they spent most of their visit talking about Holliston."

From the *Holliston Servicemen's News* – April 1945:

"T/5 Alfred Kampersal attached to Quarter Master Truck Company in Patton's Third Army met Phillip Wilder – Merchant Mariner of Holliston, while he was stationed in Liege. He is now somewhere in France."

Bill Hamlet on the right, wearing blazer

From the *Holliston Servicemen's News* – November 1944:

"Bill Hamlet Seaman 2/C enlisted June 15 and after his training at Sampson, New York he was sent to Shoemaker, California. He is now located at Coronado, San Diego, California, training in the amphibious forces."

As a member of the local American Legion, Hamlet would help bring the USMC Band (the President's Own) to town from Washington, D.C., twice for a concert. A member of the town's 250th anniversary committee in 1974, Hamlet was a long-time assessor for the town. He would pass away from a heart attack while addressing town meeting at the age of 59 in 1985.

Doug Brown

Staff Sgt. Doug Brown served in Belgium during World War II with the 942nd Airborne as a topographer. Loading duffle bags on his way home, Brown decided to load his last so that when he arrived home his bag would be first off. That bag loaded with gifts was stolen and his bride-to-be Sally Robshaw would go without. Brown served the town as building inspector for twenty years before retiring in 1986. Rarely did Brown ever miss marching in a Memorial Day parade.

Harry Sands

Having seen action in the New Guinea area and later in the Philippines, Staff Sgt. Harry Sands, husband of Carol Shelnut, would be killed in action on May 22, 1945 on the island of Mindoro. Sands was an aerial gunner on a B-24 Army bomber. His memorial square is located at the intersection of Fiske and Central Streets. He is buried at Long Island National Cemetery.

Dorrance White

Dorrance White's family moved to Holliston during the Great Depression. The family lived in an abandoned cabin in the woods near Miller Hill and the quarries, down a dirt road across from Prospect Street. The family eventually moved from the woods to a house on Highland Street not far from the rural dirt road. Lt. Dorrance White was a member of the Army Air Forces 514th Bomber Squadron, 376th Bomber Group and was lost in action on July 8, 1944. He is memorialized at Florence American Cemetery, on Via Cassia, outside the city of Florence, Italy. White was a member of Holliston High School Class of 1939. White's father Arnold began building swing sets in his Highland Street garage and the company would become ChildLife. The elder White set up a swing set for President John Kennedy's children, Caroline and John, at the White House in the early 1960s.

Walter Murphy

Navy veteran Walter Murphy would arrive in England on St. Patrick's Day, March 17, 1944. One year later he married an English girl named Vera Ireland on St. Patrick's Day 1945. Ireland's parents were fond of saying about the Americans, "You're overpaid, oversexed, and over here". Murphy returned to the US with his new war bride and served in the Naval Reserve. He would be called up again for the Korean War and served on the *USS Hamul.* Active in the local VFW Post 8507, Murphy is pictured at a Memorial Day service and his wife Vera stands in front of him.

John P. Handy

John P. Handy was a member of the Eighty-fifth Cavalry Recon Squadron, Fifth Armored Division, Mechanized. His unit liberated Le Merle-sur-Sarthe, France the day prior to Handy being killed in action on August 12, 1944. John Handy is buried at Brittany American Cemetery, St. James, France. His memorial square is located at Franklin and Norfolk Streets.

Victor Laronga

While our book focuses on Hollistonians either native or long time residing, Vic Laronga was neither.

Vic was a Mendon resident and Holliston's town barber. Born in Italy and arriving in the United States at age 14 months, Laronga served in the Army's Sixty-fourth Engineer Topographic Company and helped map out the invasion of Iwo Jima. Stationed in Guam, Tech-5 Sgt. Laronga would also serve as part of the occupation army in Japan once the war ended. Opening his barber shop adjacent to Pete's Restaurant, (the Black Horse at the time in 1946), Laronga retired in 2000 at age 80. In 1992 the town honored Laronga by making him the parade marshal for the annual Memorial Day parade.

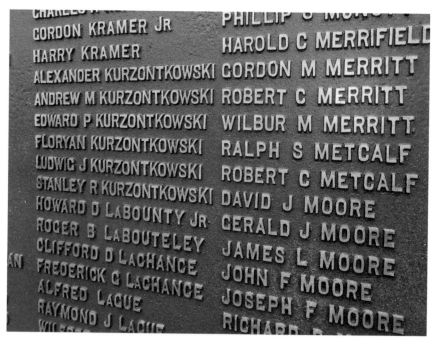

World War II honor roll at town hall

From the *Holliston Servicemen's News* – November 1944 –
"Local Scenes":

"Jimmy Inches peering up and down the street for customers.

Behind a cloud of smoke, Charlie Williams giving someone the latest scandal.

'Tootie' Quitt and his 'Sorry – No Gas' sign on the pumps.

The new fishing (deep sea) firm of Joe Phipps, Henry Norris, Cy Goodrich and Sarg Eldracher telling the world why they didn't catch any fish.

Herman Bailey trying out his stock of armchairs on the sidewalk with Ted Leland.

'Ma' Boardman on her regular morning shopping and 'you tell 'em' journey.

Damigella looking for speeders up by the church cemetery.

Tony the barber on the lookout for whiskers, long hair and hot tips.

The regulars in and out of Scanlon's Black Horse for sinkers and java.

Alexander's rapid delivery truck now blushing in a new coat of fiery red paint.

'Dolly' Bray's genial 'Hi, there' to all who pass the door.

'Bricky' Hamlet at 10:30 a.m. getting an early start.

Both drug stores closed Sunday and Wednesday afternoons.

What do you know – the old Williams delivery covered wagon is now out, and a new beach wagon has taken its place.

On your return home, the chance of seeing double is becoming greater every day – Ray Finn is the proud Pop of twin sons.

John Turner has renovated the old blacksmith shop and is now established as a machine shop.

Holliston High boys have organized an independent football team this fall. Played the Braggville team last week and did a good job – won b'gosh.

Howard Vernon

From the *Holliston Servicemen's News* – May-June 1945:

"Howard 'Punk' Vernon, Specialist G, 3/C has arrived home from Bahia, Brazil, on a 30 day furlough, after an absence of 15 months. He has been in the service for three years, having spent sixteen months of that time studying gunnery in Newfoundland. He made the trip of 7,000 miles by Navy air transport, making the flight in two days."

Vernon was a high school standout athlete and played semi-pro baseball on the West Coast after the war.

M. Vincent Connolly

Vinny Connolly's family hailed from Tubbercurry County, Sligo, Ireland and the family operated a farm on Prospect Street. Sgt. Connolly would serve in the US Army in Rio de Janeiro, Brazil training personnel of the Brazilian Air Force. In civilian life Connolly retired as the assistant postmaster of Holliston in the 1980s.

Harry Kramer

Harry Kramer told his daughter that he recalled his mother waving to him as he left Breezy Hills Farm on Adams Street for service in World War II in Europe. Kramer was worth his weight in gold since he understood German, as he was fluent in Dutch, a similar language.

Masthead from Holliston Servicemen's News

From the *Holliston Servicemen's News,* November 1944 – "Briefs About The Boys":

"Cpl. Larry Porter returned to Camp Crowder, Missouri, after two weeks furlough and is now at Fort Leonard Wood, Missouri, waiting to go overseas.

T. Cpl. Phillip L. Roberts, after thirty-three months in the southwest Pacific, was home on a twenty-one day furlough, and has gone to Ashville, North Carolina for a two week period.

Holliston lost another civilian this week. Hollis Gallot left Tuesday, after having volunteered for induction. Roger Labouteley, Ph, M. 2/C made the news. The newspapers carried radioed news of his performing an amputation of a wounded Marine's leg under heavy fire and flame-throwers during the battle of Guam last July.

Five of the Scanlon boys are now in the service. Four in the Navy and one in the Army.

Sgt. George Mantell is still in Italy, and had a very interesting visit to Rome.

Bill Hamlet S 2/C enlisted June 15 and after his boot training at Sampson, New York, he was sent to Shoemaker, California.

As most of you probably know, Pvt. Arthur Chapin was taken Prisoner of War by Germany during the Italian campaign.

Cpl. Henry Holbrook is still tearing around England on his English bike, smoking English cigars and loving English girls.

Mr. and Mrs. Charles Pidgeon of Quincy Place have identified a soldier in the roto-gravure section of a Boston Sunday paper as their son, Pvt. Charles Pidgeon, Jr. The picture shows American GIs somewhere in France, bringing in German prisoners on the double at the point of a rifle. Pvt. Pideon is known to be serving with the infantry in that sector.

Bill Sheehan, captain of the Y.O. 107, a navy oiler attached to a task force in the South Pacific, recently met Ned Wise, Jerry Kennedy and Walter Rossini.

Sgt. John Sheehan is stationed in India, flying on a B-20.

Everett Blair, Wilbur Blair and Harold Angerman met and had a little chat somewhere in the southwest Pacific area.

Pvt. William Honey was home for two weeks from Camp Shelby, Missouri in September.

T/5 Thomas Honey was reported wounded in France, August 22. Tom is still recovering in a hospital in England. His nephew, Donald, who was wounded while on a mine sweeper during the invasion in France, is in the same hospital. To make the picture complete, Tom's sister, Martha, an army nurse, is on duty at the same institution.

PFC Alfred Kampersal, Engineers Aviation Battalion, and Pvt. Ralph Sherman, Q.M. Truck Corps met in France and report they spent most of their visit talking about Holliston.

A reunion of the two sons of Mr. and Mrs. Michael Hayes was held in September, after a separation of over 3 years. Paul is the eldest son, is in the Army, and Joseph is in the Navy.

T/3 Andrew W. Kurzontkowski is now stationed in France with Patton's Third Army."

Warren "Presty" Bresnahan

From the *Holliston Servicemen's News*, January 1945:

"Warren Bresnahan TM 1/C, on board the *USS Lansdowne* writes that the only person from home that he has run into is Philip Fales SF 3/C on the tender *USS Prairie*. 'News flash' - just received word that Warren met Walter Rossini onboard an aircraft carrier the other day."

Warren Bresnahan served both in the Atlantic with the US Navy aboard the *USS Kearney* and later in the Pacific. Bresnahan would be responsible for escorting Japanese officials out to the *USS Missouri* in Tokyo Bay on September 2, 1945 for the surrender of Japan.

Leroy Robshaw

From the *Holliston Servicemen's News,* March 1945:

"Leroy W. Robshaw, USN, has been promoted to the rank of chief yeoman. He is serving aboard an LST in the South Pacific. He recently paid a visit to Curtis Claflin aboard an aircraft carrier at one of the island bases there."

Robshaw would be the longtime quartermaster for VFW Post 8507.

Bert Gates

Bert Gates and his brother Clarence would run an automotive repair station next to the East Holliston Fire Station. Bert was the longtime finance officer for the local American Legion Post 47. Gates was known to carry all the post's monies around in a cigar box.

Thomas Munn

Thomas Munn, USMC, would be killed in action on November 20, 1943 in the first day of a three-day battle at Tarawa Atoll in the Gilbert Islands. In support of the battle, the US Navy's flotilla included seventeen aircraft carriers, twelve battleships, eight heavy cruisers, four light carriers, and sixty-six destroyers. Munn's memorial square is located at Linden and Woodland Streets.

Lawrence Porter

From the Holliston Servicemen's News, April 1945:

"Great News! Staff Sgt. Lawrence S. Porter, reported missing in action, was liberated from a German prison hospital after having had his left foot amputated at the ankle, and has already arrived here from a hospital in France. He is now in England Central Hospital at Atlantic City, New Jersey. And is only waiting until he can get out on that famed boardwalk. Welcome home, Larry."

Porter would go on to own the first liquor license in town for his shop, Depot Liquors.

Will Brigham

From the Holliston Servicemen's News, December 1944:

"Lt. Bill Brigham wrote that he saw Joe Rudnick in Germany. He was a treat to look at with two weeks beard, up to his neck in mud, tommy gun over his shoulder, and smoking a pipe. He tried the best to catch his attention but Joe got away before Bill could get him."

Brigham would go on to run prisoner of war camp #D in Cherbourg for captured Germans. A member of the 120th Infantry Regiment, Thirtieth Infantry Division, Brigham made friends with a German POW and corresponded with him for years after the war had ended.

George Blair

From the Holliston Servicemen's News, April 1945:

"George Blair has earned his rating of Radarman, 2/C, after completing his training at San Pedro, California. He is now stationed on the *USS Foote.* George met Henry Holmes just after the invasion of Luzon and they had quite a chat. He has been in the same port as Bob Scanlon but they never did get together."

Henry Holmes

Henry Holmes was aboard the *USS Baine* on May 27, 1945, when the destroyer was hit in quick succession by two Japanese suicide kamikaze planes. The first hit forward seriously damaged the bridge, and the second hit amidships blew the number two funnel overboard and demolished the amidships superstructure. Holmes was below deck and was surrounded by fire. He forever lived with a healthy fear of fire. Ironically, Holmes would be promoted to chief fire controlman in July of 1945.

Curtis Claflin

Curtis "Cactus" Claflin would serve in the US Navy in the Pacific, where he met several more Holliston men. A long-time employee of the Holliston Water Department, Claflin moved to the West Coast in retirement.

John Mahoney

Seaman 2/C John Mahoney died on April 9, 1942 of pneumonia at Newport, Rhode Island. World War II was a family affair; all three Mahoney brothers served.

From the Holliston Servicemen's News, February 1945:

"Robert Mahoney, T/M, 1/C and Gloria Morse were married at Hunters Point, California, on January 6. Gloria will return to Holliston after Bob puts out to sea again, early in March. Cpl. Paul Mahoney has received his certificate as a qualified parachutist, from the US Army Parachute School. Paul is at P.O.E., awaiting orders."

John Mahoney's memorial square is located at Washington and Pearl Streets.

Francis Finn

Francis Finn served as part of Patton's Third Army in Europe. Finn came from a farming family. A portion of their family land on Hollis Street would be taken by the town by eminent domain to erect a new high school in the late 1960s. Francis and his brother Raymond would operate Finn Brothers Mobil Station at the corner of Concord and Washington Streets. With a gruff demeanor, Francis was actually a sheep in wolf's clothing.

Charles H. Carroll

Lt. Charles Carroll, better known as "Tip" was a battalion surgeon's assistant in the medical detachment of the 115th Infantry in Germany. He wrote home that he had the thrill of his life when he met his brother-in-law, Sgt. Robert A. Young, in Holland. They had not seen each other since Tip went into the Army four years earlier. When in France, Carroll wrote that he met Charlie Bontili and it was great to talk over old times with a friend from home.

Roy Jensen

After graduation from Boston College in 1934, Roy took his flight training in Pensacola, Florida in 1935 and served on the aircraft carriers *USS Ranger* and *USS Saratoga*.

He left the US Navy as a Lt. j.g. after four years of service and began working for Pan American Airways (PAA) on July 27, 1939 until he retired as an airline captain on July 31, 1972. Roy passed away April 8, 1997 in San Diego.

From the Holliston Servicemen's News, November 1944:

"Capt. Roy Jensen A.T.C. is now flying a hospital ship between Miami and the war theater. Previous to this run, Roy was flying the Army Cannon Ball out of Miami to Karachi, India. On this run he often stopped at Ascension Island and there spent time with Cpl. Gordon Chesmore."

Ralph Sherman

From his obituary:

"Ralph 'Mike' Norman Sherman, 95, died peacefully on the afternoon of Tuesday, October 25, 2016 with family by his side at Rackleff Place in Canby, Oregon. Ralph was born in Holliston (Braggville), Massachusetts on August 22, 1921, to the late George Metcalf and Gertrude McCue Sherman. Ralph helped on the fox farm and, later, took the night shift in the locomotive roundhouses, keeping the fires burning. He figure-skated on frozen cranberry bogs and danced at his parents' regular barn dances. A member of a washtub band called The Hillbillies, playing harmonica always remained part of his identity. He also restored and exhibited award-winning antique cars. Ralph served in the 852nd Engineering Aviation Battalion supporting the Eighty-second Airborne in Europe during World War II, building airfields. Their final achievement was the repair of Tempelhof airport runway in Berlin."

Roy Hulbert

From the Holliston Servicemen's News, March 1945:

"Roy Hulbert AMM 2/C reports from Trinidad that he is well pleased with the climate and finds the food to be very good."

After the war Hulbert would operate Hulbert Orchards in the Lowland, Regal, Norland Streets area. Hulbert would also serve for a period as the town's highway superintendent and as a member of the fire department on Engine #3 in East Holliston.

Dan Turner

From the Holliston Servicemen's News:

"PFC Dan Turner writes that he reached his outfit just in time to come through the last campaign of the Elbe River with them. Dan said it would have done us good to see these Supermen giving up by the thousands two days after they made the crossing. Dan wrote his letter with a 'looted' German typewriter, bemoaning the fact that the Jerries don't put the keys in the same place as a US machine. Dan's division, the 82nd has been chosen to represent the US troops in the city of Berlin, so we'll be glad to hear later about your marching down the 'Unter den Linden,' Dan."

Everett Blair

From the Holliston Servicemen's News:

"Everett Blair, MM 1/C, aboard the *USS Hailey,* writes that he has taken part in nine major invasions; Kawajalein, Eniwetok, Saipan, Guam, Palau, Ulitki, Leyte, Lingaye Gulf, and Iwo Jima." Blair would join the Merchant Marines after World War II and remain in the Naval Reserves until the Korean War.

Clarence Robshaw

From the Holliston Servicemen's News, January 1945:

"Clarence W. Robshaw, Radarman 1/C, USN, son of Mr. and Mrs. Clarence Robshaw of 58 Front Street, is on a thirty-one day leave at his home after eighteen months in the European theater. He wears four stars for four major engagements on the FTO ribbon, one of which is for his service on an LST during the Normandy invasion. He will report to New York for further assignment."

Robshaw worked for "Ma" Bell until his retirement.

Richard Kampersal

Richard "Itsy" Kampersal leads the US Army Band in Korea.
From a long line of brothers who all settled on South Street in
Holliston near the family farm, Kampersal Dairy, in the
Braggville section of town, the Kampersal boys would also serve
many years manning Holliston Fire Department's Engine #4,
which was literally stationed in their front yards.

Vincent Mullen

Sgt. Vincent Mullen, 22, of 20 Prospect Street would be the first Holliston man wounded in Korea, in 1951. Mullen was a sophomore at Massachusetts College of Pharmacy when he was called to military duty. Mullen would complete his pharmacy training and serve as a pharmacist at McKeen's Drug Store here in town and later work in Franklin. He raised his family on Prospect Street.

John Clancy on left, taking a break with a buddy from the rigors of war

John Clancy would serve in Korea in 1951-1952 with the
516th Infantry Regiment, Company H, 101st Airborne Division.
Clancy returned home and worked as a stockbroker for
Hornblower and Weeks and Dean Witter and Reynolds. With his
wife Patricia Gillon they raised their four children on Oakridge
Road. Clancy passed away in 2014. John was the son of
Holliston's last country doctor who would make house calls, Dr.
Leo Clancy.

William Maguire

Bill Maguire of Mudville would serve with the US Army in Korea. A Draper Corporation employee, Maguire moved south when the Hopedale plant closed, only to return to his Holliston roots in retirement. Bill earned the silver bowl for "the best beard" at Holliston's 250th Anniversary beard judging contest in 1974.

Henry Dellicker

Henry Dellicker and his bride Jackie arrived in Holliston in 1958. Between 1950 and 1960 the town's population would grow 65%, from 3,753 to 6,222.

Dellicker served shore duty in Korea in 1953 before being assigned to the *USS Bairoko* and witnessing the first test of a hydrogen bomb in Bikini Atoll in 1954. "I hope never to see or experience anything like these tests again," he said afterward. Dellicker would go on to serve aboard the *USS Hornet* and *USS Essex*.

A 2003 Holliston Citizen of the Year, "Hank" has literally served on every elected and appointed board in town with the exception of the finance and school committees. A life of service to country and town that few ever achieve.

*War dog retraining facility at 55 Prospect Street,
1950 and 2021*

Operated after the war, the property at 55 Prospect Street was used as a training facility to re-purpose dogs used by the military during World War II. The black and white photo is from a 1950 book titled *Teach Your Dog Obedience*. Robert Moore of South Natick was a dog trainer at the facility. Moore, the holder of a Distinguished Flying Cross, was a POW in Europe, coincidentally in the same POW camp as Holliston's Lou Paltrineri, the former owner of Fiske's General Store. Moore would fancy the girl across the street from 55 Prospect Street, Linda Connolly, and they married. While the property was fenced in, the war dogs would often intimidate passersby along the street and the facility closed by 1950. The property was purchased in 1950 by Maj. Joe Kempton, himself a World War II veteran.

John Chase

John Chase was a graduate of Holliston High. Chase served with Company B, First Battalion, Twenty-sixth Marines, Third Marine Division. A lance corporal, Chase was a rifleman and was killed in action on June 7, 1967 on Hill 800, Khe Sanh, Quang Tri Province, Vietnam. His death was little remembered in Holliston at the time as his parents had moved to Laurel, Maryland. Chases' memorial square lies at the corner of Norfolk and Clark Streets, near his childhood home.

David Purington

A graduate of Holliston High in 1968, David Purington would join the Navy in 1973. Lt. Cmdr. Purington served twenty years as a naval officer and instructor of fixed wing aircraft and helicopters. He served as a Special Forces squadron leader for a mine sweeping naval unit with tours of duty in Southeast Asia, the Mediterranean Sea, Suez Canal, and Desert Storm. He served aboard the *USS Inchon, USS Trenton,* and *USS Eisenhower.* Purington passed away in 1996 and is buried at Lake Grove Cemetery.

Clifford LaChance

Sgt. First Class Clifford LaChance saw service with the Merchant
Marines before joining the Army in 1948. A Jennings Road
resident, LaChance would serve with the Forty-fifth Mechanized
Calvary in the Canal Zone, before a tour with the
Second Infantry in Korea. A career soldier, LaChance would
serve in Germany with the Twelfth Infantry before being
stationed with MACV (Military Assistance Command Vietnam).
LaChance was killed in action on August 7, 1966. LaChance's
memorial square stands at Gooch's Corner, the intersection of
Concord and Ashland Streets.

Police Color Guard

The Holliston Police Department Color Guard is pictured lined up on Exchange Street in the late 1970s for the annual Memorial Day parade. Military veterans from left to right: Norm Gillen, Donald Haynes, a Vietnam veteran, John Johnson, and Bruce McKinnon. Johnson would tragically lose his life after making a traffic stop in East Holliston on August 13, 1981.

Jim Carbino

This photo is one of the few in Jim Carbino's possession due to a previous house fire when he lost all his belongings. Carbino is a Holliston resident and a graduate of Marian High in Framingham. Jim would serve from 1967-1968 with the Second of the 187th, 101 Airborne (Screaming Eagles) in Vietnam. Carbino sustained an injury when he stepped on a punji stick booby trap, for which he had several toes amputated. After the war Carbino owned and operated the Village Pub in the Metcalf section of town from 1970-1980.

American Legion Auxiliary

The American Legion Auxiliary was open to spouses and children and grandchildren of American Legion members. Pictured left to right are, Marion Hudson, Margaret Foster (a World War II veteran), and Tina Blaney.

Fifty-year continuous members of the
American Legion Post 47

Celebrating 50 years of continuous membership in the local Legion Post 47, and all World War II veterans, are, front row left to right: Stan Olmsted, Donald (Bud) Rawson, and Everett Blair. Back row, left to right: Bill Murphy, Ed and Frank Serocki, Don Bolin, and Bobby Moore. These veterans have all passed away and as of this writing, only fourteen World War II veterans remain alive in town.

Michael Sullivan

Specialist Sullivan was born in San Diego, California and grew up in Holliston. He enlisted in the Army in January 2005. He attended basic combat training at Fort Knox, Kentucky and advanced individual training at Aberdeen Proving Ground as a 44B/metal worker. Upon completion he reported to Fort Drum, New York serving as a metal worker and heavy wheeled service and recovery operator with B Company. 10th Brigade Support Battalion, First Brigade Combat Team, Tenth Mountain Division. He did one tour at Camp Liberty, Iraq in support of Operation Iraqi Freedom from 2005-2006. Sullivan's Holliston military roots stretch back to his great grandparents, Steve Honey, a World War I veteran, and his wife Orrie, who operated Friendly Taxi Service from their 70 Central Street home.

*Elin Austin and Roger Gandini hang a poster for a coalition
troop killed in Iraq*

Between the years of 2003-2019, the American Legion Post 47
hung posters each Memorial and Veterans Day to honor the lives
lost in the Iraq and Afghanistan Wars. In 2005 the posters were
hung for the losses up to that date, resulting in the length of the
tribute stretching into the main streets of six abutting towns for
a distance of 34.4 miles. A two-day Nor'easter tore the posters
from the utility poles and the tribute thereafter was downsized
to honor those from the previous six months who had lost their
lives. In all, the handwritten posters listing rank, name, age, and
home state or country totaled 8,479 – or 16,958 as they were
double-sided. Roger Gandini, a former National Guardsman,
was the man who donated the poster board for the entire
seventeen years the tribute was held.

Matt Hepfinger

Matt Hepfinger is pictured with his family

Lt. Cdr. Matt Hepfinger is a 2003 graduate of Holliston High and 2007 graduate of the United States Naval Academy. He also holds an MBA from the University of Florida. Upon commissioning, Matt entered flight training and earned his wings as a naval aviator in 2008. He has deployed worldwide flying the P-3C Orion and P-8A Poseidon.

George and Nicholas Snow

George "Dave" Snow served twenty active duty years with the US Navy, first as an electronics teacher in Boston and later aboard the *USS Goodrich* off the coast of Korea. Snow would also serve aboard the submarine *USS Daniel Webster.* After his military service, Snow worked for the Cleveland Institute of Electronics. Pictured with his grandson Nicholas, the younger Snow would serve two tours of duty in Afghanistan in Army ordinance. Nicholas currently works for the US government in security.

Veterans pose on town hall steps

Each year since 2006, Holliston veterans gather for a Veterans Day (November 11) ceremony at town hall and enjoy a meal in upper town hall afterwards. Gathered for this photo are veterans of World War II, Korea, Vietnam, Panama, Grenada, Desert Storm, Afghanistan, and Iraq.

Jackie (Hepfinger) Franc

Lt. Jackie (Hepfinger) Franc is a 2009 graduate of Holliston High School and a 2013 graduate of The Ohio State University. Upon commissioning, Jackie entered flight school and earned her Wings of Gold as a naval aviator in 2015. She has deployed multiple times in the Pacific Area Of Responsibility and flies the MH-60S helicopter.

Bobby Blair

About the Author

Bobby Blair is a homegrown Hollistonian. His paternal side is traced back via DNA to Scotland and Jean Francois, the first Blair of the Blairs, around the year 1190. His maternal ancestors hail from Ireland and settled in Holliston's Mudville neighborhood during the Irish Potato Famine of the 1840s. Bobby served with the Army's First Field Forces, Fifty-second Artillery Group, Seventh Battalion Fifteenth Field Artillery Regiment in An Khe and Pleiku, Vietnam. A past commander for both the local American Legion Post 47 and VFW Post 8507, Blair retired from the Holliston Post Office after thirty-seven years as a letter carrier in 2005.

Blair is known locally as the "Mayor of Mudville," having initiated the first Mudville block party in 1981. He was named a "Holliston Citizen of the Year" in 1997 and *MetroWest Daily News* "Man of the Year" in 2005. In 2005, Blair began writing for Mary Greendale's *Holliston Net News* and several years later formed the *Holliston Reporter* with fellow colleagues Bill Tobin and Paul Saulnier. For the past 15 years, Blair has farmed on Highland Street in Holliston, growing dahlias as a main crop. Combining his interest in writing and veterans affairs, *A Holliston Oath to Support and Defend* preserves for future generations the names and faces of those who have passed our way.